USBORNE HOTSHOTS

HAIR PLAITING

USBORNE HOTSHOTS
HAIR PLAITING

Fiona Watt and Lisa Miles

Consultant: Jacki Wadeson
Hair stylist: Kathleen Bray

Edited by Cheryl Evans
Designed by Helen Westwood

Illustrated by Chris Chaisty
Photographs by Ray Moller

Series editor: Judy Tatchell
Series designer: Ruth Russell

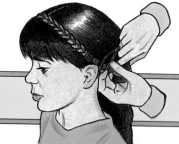

CONTENTS

Simple plait

It only takes a little practice to be good at plaiting. Here you can see how to plait the simplest, three-strand plait.

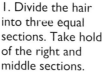

You will need: brush, comb, a covered band.

1. Divide the hair into three equal sections. Take hold of the right and middle sections.

2. Cross your hands so that the right section of hair comes over the middle one and they swap places.

3. Hold the new right section between your thumb and first finger and the middle one in your other fingers.

4. Cross the left section over the middle one. Take it in your right fingers. Swap the middle one to your left hand.

5. Now, cross the right section over the middle one again. Swap it over to the fingers of your left hand.

6. Take the left section over the middle one, swapping it to the fingers of your right hand as you do it.

7. Continue plaiting down the hair by crossing the right section, then the left one, over the middle section.

8. When you have plaited right to the ends of all the sections of hair, hold the ends firmly between your first finger and thumb.

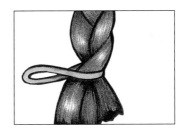

9. Take a covered band and slip it over the end of the plait. Twist it around once to form a small loop at one side.

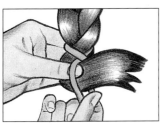

10. Put your fingers through the loop and pull the hair through, swapping the loop to your other hand.

You could knot a bright scarf around your hair.

11. If the band is still loose, twist and pull the hair through again. You may need to do this several times.

Ribbon braid

It's easy to plait ribbons through your hair. You can buy lots of different kinds from department stores.

You will need: covered band, three ribbons 15cm (6in) longer than your hair, hair clip.

Use ribbons which aren't too wide as they are easier to plait.

Choose ribbons which match your clothes.

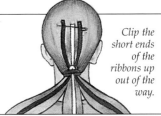

1. Lay the ribbons on top of each other. Tie them in a knot 10cm (4in) from one end. Gather your hair into a low ponytail. Secure it with a band.

2. Slip the ribbons under one of the loops in the band. Make sure that the knot is above the band. Divide the hair into three sections, each with a ribbon.

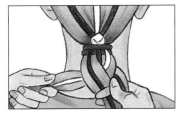

3. Hold each piece of ribbon tightly against its own section of hair as you plait. Try not to let the ribbons twist as you cross the sections over.

4. Continue to plait to the ends of the sections. Secure the hair and ribbons with a covered band. Tie two of the loose ribbon ends around the band.

5. Unclip the short ends which are clipped to the back of the head. Cross two of the ribbons under the plait, then tie them neatly over the covered band.

Tip

Use sharp scissors to cut the ends of the ribbons on a slant before you plait them. This stops them from fraying.

Tiara plait

You can achieve a pretty effect by plaiting a small section of hair then crossing it over the top of your head.

You will need:
small covered band, hair clip.

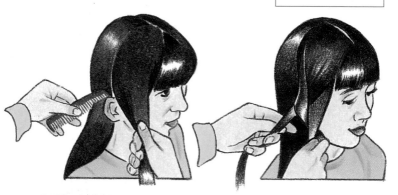

1. Comb the hair and make a middle parting. Take a front section of hair and hold it near to the top of your ear.

2. Divide this hair into three equal sections. Plait your hair, keeping the ends pulled downward all the time.

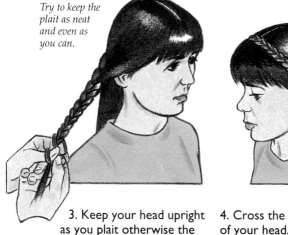

Try to keep the plait as neat and even as you can.

3. Keep your head upright as you plait otherwise the plait won't be even. Secure the end with a covered band.

4. Cross the plait over the top of your head, so that the end lies just behind your ear. Secure it with a hair clip.

Brush the loose hair carefully over the clip to hide it.

Tip

Snap hair clips are really good for securing the end of a thin plait under loose hair. They are also very useful for clipping loose hair out of the way while you are plaiting another section (see mini plaits on pages 30-31).

Clips like these don't fall out of your hair easily.

French princess

This style isn't plaited, but is an easy way to make an effect rather like a French plait (see page 12).

You will need: four fabric bands.

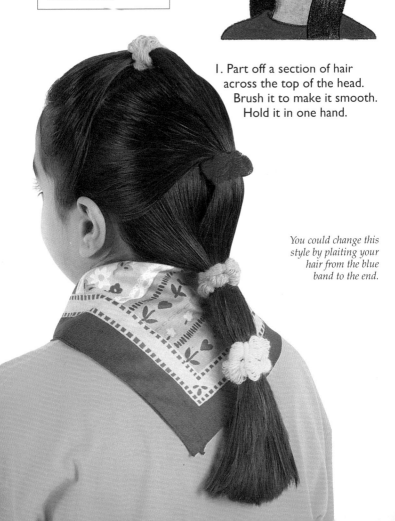

1. Part off a section of hair across the top of the head. Brush it to make it smooth. Hold it in one hand.

You could change this style by plaiting your hair from the blue band to the end.

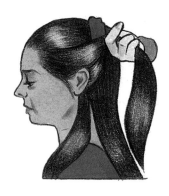

2. Twist a fabric band around this section of hair until it is tight. You could wear your hair like this if you want.

3. Lay the section down on the loose hair. Pick up a new section from behind the ears. Secure it with another band.

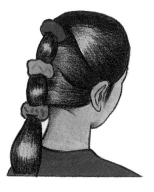

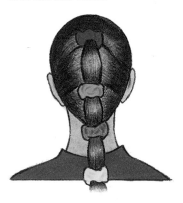

4. Gather all the hair together into a ponytail and secure it with another band at the top of your neck.

5. Attach a fourth band at the bottom of the hair. Adjust the bands to make them evenly spaced, if you need to.

You can use any kind of covered band for this style.

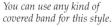

French plait

You'll need a little practice to do a neat French plait, but once you have mastered the technique, you'll find they are quite quick and easy.

> **You will need:**
> a covered band.

1. Pick up and pull back a section of hair from the front of your head. Divide it in three and plait the strands once.

2. Use one of your fingers to pick up a thin strand from the loose hair next to the right section, at the front.

3. Join the strand in neatly with the right section. Cross this strand over the middle one in the normal way.

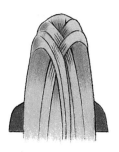

4. Take a thin strand from the hair on the left. Join it in neatly with the left strand, as before. Plait it over the middle one.

5. Take another thin strand from the loose hair on the right and join it in with the right section. Plait it.

6. Pick up and join another strand of loose hair in with the left section. Then, plait it over the middle section.

Pull each strand firmly as you plait to keep the plait neat.

Gather up all the fine hair at the neck.

7. Continue plaiting tightly in this way, taking a strand of hair from each side of your head to join in with the plait.

8. At your neck, divide the remaining hair into two sections and join them into the left and right sections.

9. Plait the three strands of hair in the normal way to the end and secure the plait with a covered band.

Short French plait

This style is one which you can plait even if your hair is quite short. You can also do it if your hair is long.

You will need:
a covered band.

Plait back along your head, not down.

1. Make a parting. Pick up a section of hair between your ear and your forehead. Divide it in three and plait it once.

Use a small scrunchie to hide the covered band in this plait.

2. Take a thin strand from the hair below and join it to the bottom strand. Plait this strand over the strand in the middle.

3. Now pick up a thin strand from the loose hair beside the top strand and join it into the strand. Plait it over the middle.

4. Repeat steps 2 and 3 once more. Try to keep the plait as tight against your head, and as neat as you can, without pulling your hair too much.

Plait the hair downward now.

5. Now plait the three strands in the normal way to the end. Secure the plait with a covered band. Add a ribbon or a fabric scrunchie to hide it.

Crown plait

Once you can do a French plait (see pages 12-13), you can create many different styles. This crown plait is a variation of the French plait but is made across the top of your head.

You will need:
small covered band.

1. Brush your hair back from your forehead, or from the top of your fringe if you have one.

You can do this plait even if your hair is quite short.

2. Make a parting from ear to ear over your head, making a section about 7cm (3in) wide.

3. Pick up a section from over your left ear. Divide it into three equal strands and plait it once.

4. Pick up a strand from the loose hair beneath the right strand. Join it with the strand.

5. Cross the right strand over the middle. Pick up a strand and plait it in with the left strand.

6. Continue to plait over the top of the head, picking up a strand and joining it as you go.

7. When you reach the other ear, plait the loose ends of hair in the normal way. Secure with a band.

Two-plait princess

This is a variation of the French princess style on pages 10-11. You could also simply wear the plait on top of the loose hair, as it would be at the end of step 2 (see opposite page).

You will need:
two covered bands.

You could hide the covered band at the bottom of the plait with two ribbons tied together.

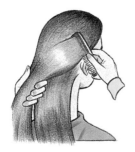

1. Brush your hair well then use a comb or your fingers to take a section of hair across the crown of your head.

2. Divide this section of hair into three equal parts and plait it to the end. Secure it with a covered band.

3. Allow the plait to fall straight down over the hair, then divide the loose hair into two equal sections, either side of the plait.

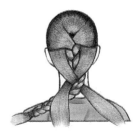

4. Plait the hair to the end, using the plait as one section and the loose hair as the other two. Secure tightly with a band.

Tying a neat bow

Loose end

Slip the ribbon through a loop of the covered band, under the plait. Tie a knot. Then make two loops, leaving two loose ends.

Now cross the loops over, with the left loop on top of the right. Bring the left loop up between the right loop and the knot. Pull the loops.

Six plaits

This elaborate style takes quite a long time to plait, but the results are fun.

You will need: one large and six small covered bands, several hair pins.

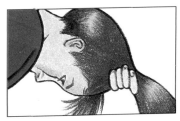

Plait this section.

Push the other sections out of the way.

1. Make a high ponytail on top of the head by bending over and grasping the hair. Secure it tightly with a covered band.

2. Divide the ponytail into six equal sections. Divide one of the sections into three and plait it. Secure the end with a band.

3. Take another section from the loose hair, roughly the same size as the first one. Divide it into three strands and plait it.

4. Repeat step 3 until you have plaited all your hair into six equal plaits. Secure each one with a covered band.

5. Hold five of the plaits above your head. Wrap the remaining plait around and around the bottom of your plaited ponytail.

6. Secure the wound plait by catching small pieces of hair with hair pins and pushing them into the middle of the plaits.

Don't leave these plaits in overnight as it's not very good for your hair and it will be uncomfortable.

Flipover

A flipover at the base of your neck can make an ordinary plait or ponytail look very stylish. You can create this style using a tool called a styler.

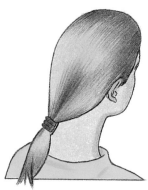

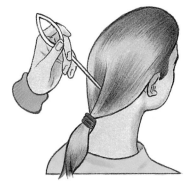

1. Brush the hair well and smooth it into a low ponytail. Secure the ponytail with a covered band.

2. Push the point of the styler carefully into the hair, just above the middle of the covered band.

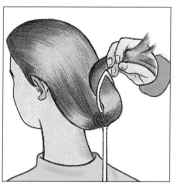

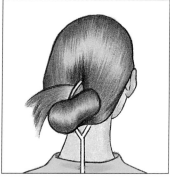

3. Lift up the ponytail and thread it through the loop of the styler. Keep holding onto the end of the ponytail.

4. Gently pull the styler downward. The ponytail will go through the hair and come out underneath.

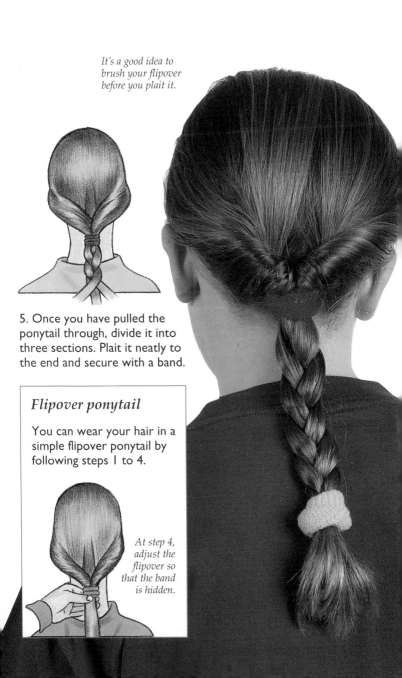

It's a good idea to brush your flipover before you plait it.

5. Once you have pulled the ponytail through, divide it into three sections. Plait it neatly to the end and secure with a band.

Flipover ponytail

You can wear your hair in a simple flipover ponytail by following steps 1 to 4.

At step 4, adjust the flipover so that the band is hidden.

Beaded plait

You can plait your hair and add beads to the end of it, even if your hair is quite short. Plastic beads are best to use because they are light, but you could use wooden or glass ones.

You will need: beads with large holes, embroidery thread.

It's not very comfortable to sleep in beads, so take them out at night.

1. Make a middle parting. Pick up a 1cm (½in) section at the parting and divide it into three strands.

2. Plait the strands neatly to about 5cm (2in) from the ends. Wet the ends and smooth them together.

3. Thread the bead onto the plait. Grip the end and push the bead up. Add one or two more beads if you want to.

4. Wind 5cm (2in) of thread several times around the end of the plait. Tie the ends of the thread in a knot.

Fishtail plait

Fishtail plaits are plaited in a different way to three-strand plaits. They look intricate but they aren't as difficult to do as they may seem. You will need someone to help you with this style.

1. Use a comb to make a parting down the back of the head so that you have two equal sections.

Add a ribbon or a scrunchie to cover the band at the end of your fishtail.

2. Hold the hair in your left hand as shown. Pick up a thin strand from the outside of the right section.

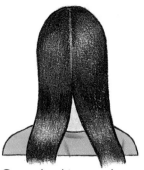

3. Cross the thin strand over and join it into the inside of the left section of hair. Smooth it in with this section.

4. Swap the sections of hair to your right hand and take a fine strand from the outside of the left section.

5. Cross the strand over to join the inside of the right section. Smooth it in tidily with the hair of this section.

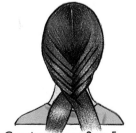

6. Continue steps 2 to 5, working down the plait. Keep the thickness of the fine strands even as you plait.

7. When you reach the bottom of the hair, hold the ends of the hair tightly and secure the plait with a covered band.

Knotted bunches

You can create lots of different styles once you have plaited your hair. To do this style, you simply tie your plaited bunches into big knots.

You will need:
two covered bands.

To wear your hair in this style you need to plait your hair quite loosely, starting level with your ears.

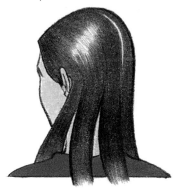

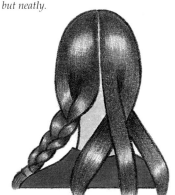

1. Use a comb to make a middle parting. Push one side of your hair out of the way, then divide the other side into three equal sections.

2. Plait the three sections to the end but make the plait very loose. Secure it tightly with a covered band. Do the same to the other side.

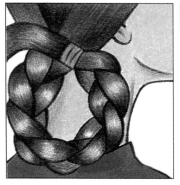

3. Hold the end of one plait and make a big loop by pulling the end up towards your ear. Cross this end right over the top of the plait.

4. Tie the plait in a loose knot by pulling the end through the loop. Tie the other plait in the same way. Make each knot tight by pulling on the ends.

Mini plaits

Although this style takes quite a long time to plait, the results are worth it. You can leave the plaits in for several days and when you untie them you'll have amazing crinkly hair.

You will need: 16 small covered bands, hair clips.

1. Make a middle parting, then make another one down to your ear. Make a third parting going back level with your eyebrows.

2. Divide the section you have made at the front into two. Plait each section to the end of the hair. Secure each one tightly with a band.

3. Lay the two plaits you have done over the top of your head. Comb the section of hair beneath these plaits. Plait it to the end and secure it.

4. Take the parting around from above your ear to the back of your head. Divide the hair in two and plait each section, securing them tightly.

Put all the top plaits over your head.

5. Make another parting level with your ear around to the back parting. Divide the section you have made in two and plait each one.

6. Clip the last two plaits you finished onto the top of your head. Plait the remaining section of hair which is still left between your ear and the back parting.

7. Unclip all the plaits you have finished and let them hang down freely around your head. Plait all your hair on the other side of your head in the same way.

Index

With special thanks to: Luke Ashby, Jahanara Chaudhri, Charlotte Crittenden, Emily and Hannah Kirby-Jones, Marina Townsend, Francesca Tyler, Alexandra Varley-Winter, Hannah Watts and Maddie York.

This book is based on material previously published in *The Usborne Book of Plaiting and Braiding.*

First published in 1996 by Usborne Publishing Ltd., Usborne House, 83-85 Saffron Hill, London EC1N 8RT, England.

Printed in Italy.